IN LOVE AND MURDER

CRIMES OF PASSION THAT SHOCKED
THE WORLD

WILLIAM WEBB

Absolute Crime Press
ANAHEIM, CALIFORNIA

Contents

ABOUT ABSOLUTE CRIME

Absolute Crime publishes only the best true crime literature. Our focus is on the crimes that you've probably never heard of, but you are fascinated to read more about. With each engaging and gripping story, we try to let readers relive moments in history that some people have tried to forget.

Remember, our books are not meant for the faint at heart. We don't hold back--if a crime is bloody, we let the words splatter across the page so you can experience the crime in the most horrifying way!

If you enjoy this book, please visit our homepage to see other books we offer; if you have any feedback, we'd love to hear from you!

Dear reader, your heart may not be able to handle the shocking true facts presented in this humble volume. You have been warned.

INTRODUCTION

Crimes of passion have long fascinated us because they twist the most basic and desirable of emotions into evil and violence. When people kill or try to kill for love, it strikes straight to our hearts and makes us question our most basic beliefs. We like to associate love with peace and compassion, but it often generates violence.

Unlike most murderers, we can often sympathize with the perpetrators in crimes of passion. In many cases, they are the victims of callous lovers and sociopaths. At one time, French law even recognized the killing of a cheating spouse as justifiable homicide.

The emotions it raises are what make crimes of passion so hard to understand or to prosecute. Yet those emotions are what make such crimes so fascinating.

ANTONIO AGOSTINI AND THE PAJAMA GIRL

Some crimes of passion are so sensational that they can capture the imagination of an entire nation. A classic example of such a crime is Australia's legendary "Pajama Girl" mystery from the 1930s. The mystery was so engrossing that it actually diverted Australians' attention from the Great Depression that was then hitting their nation hard.

The case first attracted attention in August, 1934 when a man named Tom Griffith was moving a bull near the town of Albury, New South Wales. As he tried to lead a bull down a road, Griffith noticed something in a ditch and went to take a look. To his horror, Griffith discovered that the thing in the ditch was a woman wearing silk pajamas, hence the term Pyjama Girl (in Australia, pajama is spelled the British way with a Y). The body was soaked in kerosene and burned in an attempt to destroy evidence.

Part of the reason the case attracted so much attention was that nobody could identify the girl. Forensics wasn't very advanced in 1934, and police were unable to identify the victim. The body was even put on public display in an attempt to identify the victim. During the initial investigation, at least two missing women were listed as possible identities for the victim, Linda Agostini and Anna Philomena Morgan. Unfortunately, police couldn't make a positive identification.

The pajamas themselves added a note of sensationalism to the crime. At the time, respectable women in Australia were not supposed to wear pajamas. Silk pajamas, like those worn by the girl, were equated with loose women and prostitutes.

It Took 10 Years to Solve the Crime

Astoundingly, it took 10 years to solve the crime and bring the perpetrator to justice. The Pajama Girl's body was preserved in a tank of chemicals for future police work and stored at the University in Sydney and later at police headquarters. In 1944, the preservation work paid off when the girl in the pajamas was finally identified.

By examining dental records, investigators determined that the girl was Linda Agostini, an English immigrant who had disappeared in 1934. The identity also gave investigators a suspect, Linda's husband Antonio (or Tony) Agostini, an Italian immigrant. Agostini was arrested in Sydney and extradited to Melbourne to stand trial for murder; he and Linda had been living in Melbourne at the time of her disappearance.

Incredibly, Sydney's police commissioner William McKay knew Agostini, who had worked in the cloakroom at one of his favorite restaurants, Romanos. McKay asked Agostini to come over to his office for a chat. During the chat, Agostini confessed to the crime and made the questionable claim that he had accidently shot and killed his wife. He also admitted that he poured gasoline over the body and tried to burn it. Agostini even admitted he had moved the body to another state in an attempt to evade detection.

Antonio Agostini: Murderer or Victim of Wartime Hysteria?

Despite the confession, prosecutors were unable to convince a jury that Agostini was guilty of murder. That meant he could not hang for his crime. Instead, Agostini was convicted of manslaughter and sentenced to six years in prison. After his release, Agostini was deported to Italy, where he died in 1969.

Wartime hysteria might have played a role in Agostini's conviction. World War II was raging and Australia was in the thick of it. In 1940, Agostini and many other Italian immigrants in

Australia had been placed in internment camps after Italy declared war on the British Empire. The prejudice didn't disappear when the Italians were released in 1944.

Is the Mystery Solved or Not?

There are several big questions in the Pajama Girl case that have not been answered. The first is a motive: none was given, and even Antonio Agostini claimed not to have one.

Linda Agostini's friends and relatives gave one possible motive: they claimed Agostini was a controlling man, while Linda was something of a free spirit. Agostini had moved to Melbourne from Sydney to get Linda away from her friends before her disappearance. Another might be infidelity, and evidence suggests that Linda was promiscuous before the marriage. She may have continued cheating, which might have enraged Agostini. Since details of the couple's marriage are not available, it is impossible to verify such speculations.

Was Linda Agostini the Pajama Girl or Not?

There are even historians that doubt that Linda Agostini was the Pajama Girl. Melbourne historian Richard Evans, who has studied the case, claims the Pajama Girl had a different bust size from Linda Agostini. Evans even wrote a book listing what he claims are discrepancies in the evidence.

Even if Evans is right, it doesn't mean that Antonio Agostini was innocent. It is possible that Agostini believed that the police had found his wife's body. He might have also felt guilty and simply wanted to confess. One intriguing possibility is that Agostini murdered his wife and did such a good job of hiding her body that it was never found.

Even if Linda Agostini was not the Pajama Girl, Antonio Agostini did fit the profile of the kind of person who committed a crime of passion. He was controlling, domineering, and possibly obsessive with his wife. He wanted her all to himself, and if he couldn't have her, nobody could. It is doubtful that the truth about the Pajama Girl mystery will ever be solved, although it appears to be a classic crime of passion.

Bibliography

Australia Today . "Australia Today the Pyjama Girl Murder Case (1939)." 1939. aso.gov.au/titles/newsreels. Vintage newsreel from 1939. 21 February 2013.

DeSouza, Poppy. "Australia Today The Pyjama Girl Murder Case (1939." n.d. aso.gov.au/titles/newsreels. Curator's Notes to Vintage Newsreel from 1939. 21 February 2013.

Pennay, Bruce. "Agostini Linda (1905-1934)." n.d. http://adb.anu.edu.au/biography/agostini-linda-9966. Entry in Australian Dictionary of Biography. 21 February 2013.

Wikipedia . "Linda Agostini ." n.d. en.wikipedia.org. Online Encyclopedia Entry. 21 February 2013.

DANIEL SICKLES: THE GENERAL WHO GOT AWAY WITH MURDER

No killer in the history of the United States was more colorful or successful than Daniel Sickles. Sickles shot and killed Philip Barton Key II for having an affair with his wife in 1859 and got away with it.

Not only was Sickles the first person in the United States acquitted with the insanity defense, he went on to become a war hero, a fighting general, a successful diplomat, and a successful politician and member of Congress.

What's incredible is that Sickles did all that after shooting Key, a member of an important family who was serving as the District Attorney of Washington D.C. at the time.

Two Successful Men and a Very Sordid Affair

Daniel Sickles and Philip Barton Key were both successful men in 1859 when America was on the verge of the Civil War. Sickles was a successful politician and a former U.S. Senator who was serving in the House of Representatives. Philip Barton Key was the son of Francis Scott Key, the writer of The Star Spangled Banner, which would become America's national anthem. Key was also prominent attorney in Washington with connections to the Democratic Party.

Key was also something of a rake who liked to escort Congressmen's wives to social events. He also liked to escort the wives to his bed, a practice that eventually led to his death. Key and Sickles knew each other well: Sickles had helped get Key the appointment as District Attorney. Sickles was an important man at the time because he represented Tammany Hall, the corrupt political machine that controlled New York City in Washington.

Sometime in 1859, Key began having an affair with Sickles' young wife, Teresa. Eventually somebody, probably an enemy of Key's, sent Sickles a letter about the affair that contained the address of Key and Teresa Sickles' love nest. The news of the affair plunged Sickles into depression, then into an intense rage.

Gunned Down in the Center of Washington D.C.

Sickles sent his wife away and hatched a plan. The Congressman stationed himself in a place where he could catch Key. He then lay in wait for his target for several days with two loaded pistols.

On Feb. 27, 1859, Sickles confronted Key in Lafayette Square near the White House. When he saw the attorney, Sickles fired three times and killed Key instantly. He made no attempt to cover up the crime or hide. Not only was it committed in full view of the public, but the gunshots were so loud that President James Buchanan heard them at the White House.

Sickles then went to the home of the Attorney General of the United States, Jeremiah Black, and turned himself in. Black had Sickles arrested and taken to jail for a very comfortable stay. Sickles was kept in a comfortable apartment, rather than a cell, and he was even allowed to keep his guns. This was a fairly standard arrangement in the 19th century, as rich prisoners could easily buy special treatment from poorly paid jailers.

One of America's First Celebrity Trials

Daniel Sickles quickly became one of the first celebrity murderers in American history. His trial attracted media attention, possibly because of his political influence. Reporters watched Sickles closely and reported on his every move. National magazines covered the case and brought it into the homes of average Americans.

Sickles was charged with murder and assembled a dream team of high-paid attorneys that included Edwin M. Stanton, who later became Abraham Lincoln's Secretary of War. The attorneys concocted a novel defense they would claim Sickles was driven insane by his wife's infidelity. It was the first time the insanity defense had been used in a U.S. murder trial.

Sickles was eventually acquitted on the charges, but it is unclear if it was because of the legal strategy. More likely, his money and political influence got him off. When he was in jail on murder charges, Daniel Sickles received letters of support from many of the nation's most important politicians, including President Buchanan.

From Celebrity Killer to War Hero and General

Incredibly, Daniel Sickles retained his influence, even after getting away with murder. In 1861, he was able to get an appointment as a brigadier general of volunteers in the Union Army. Since Sickles had no military experience, the appointment was based purely on his political clout.

Oddly enough, Sickles became a very good general with an impressive war record. He fought in several of the most important battles of the Civil War, including the Peninsula Campaign, Fredericksburg, and Chancellorsville. President Lincoln was so impressed with Sickles' service at Chancellorsville that he supported his promotion to Major General.

Injuries he sustained at the battle of Gettysburg left Sickles disabled for the rest of his life. A cannonball hit his right leg while he was leading his troops. The leg had to be amputated, and Sickles' broken bone is now on display in the National Museum of Health and Medicine in Washington D.C.

An Important Man

Gettysburg made Daniel Sickles a war hero and an important figure for the rest of his life. After the war, he commanded troops occupying the southern states and undertook important diplomatic missions. At home, he held a number of important political appointments and served in Congress again. He also developed a colorful reputation overseas, and legend has it that Sickles had an affair with the Queen of Spain while serving as minister (ambassador) to that country. Another is that he tried to present a prostitute as his wife at a reception for Queen Victoria.

Daniel Sickles died in New York City in 1914 after a long and controversial career. Killing Philip Barton Key didn't seem to affect his career or his reputation at all. At the end of his life, Sickles received one of the nation's highest honors: he was buried in Arlington National Cemetery.

Bibliography

Illinois State University History of Criminal Justice . "The Washington Tragedy ." n.d. http://my.ilstu.edu/~ftmorn/cjhistory/casestud/washingt.html. Online Database Entry . 21 February 2013.

Wikipedia . "Daniel Sickles ." n.d. en.wikipedia.org. Online Encyclopedia Entry . 21 February 2013.

—. "Philip Barton Key II." n.d. en.wikipedia.org. Online Encyclopedia Entry. 21 February 2013.

DID TEXTING LEAD TO HER DEATH? THE RACHEL WADE AND SARAH LUDEMANN CASE

Deadly love triangles are actually fairly common, but they usually involve adult lovers, not texting teenaged girls and boys who work at fast food joints. Yet the love triangle between Sarah Ludemann, Joshua Camacho, and Rachel Wade involved just that. In a purely 21st century twist, the fight between Sarah Ludemann and Rachel Wade began on a social networking service and exploded into deadly reality.

The two girls from Pinellas Park, Fla. started quarreling in 2008 on MySpace – a networking service then popular with teenagers – when they discovered they were both dating the same boy. The boy was Joshua Camacho, who was working at a local Chick-fil-A franchise. The fight first spilled out into the real world over cell phones, but eventually resulted in a stabbing.

Eventually, Ludemann decided to take the fight into the real world when she drove to a house where Wade was staying. Once there, she and Wade got into a fight, which led to Ludemann's death by stabbing. The murder weapon was tossed onto a rooftop as Wade fled.

Teenaged Obsession in Cyberspace

The crime of passion was ignited by Camacho, who was definitely a louse. He was dating both girls, but let each of them believe she was his only girlfriend. This typical but callous act of male insensitivity had a terrible effect upon Rachel Wade.

Like most cheating lovers, Camacho believed he could get away with his infidelity indefinitely. He never believed that he would be detected or that his girlfriends would ever learn of his game. As what usually occurs, the girls found out about each other and a conflict ensued. Wade and Ludemann began attacking each other on MySpace and kept up the insults and taunts for months.

The triangle led to a crime of passion because Wade was obsessed with Camacho. Like most obsessed lovers, she couldn't see that she was being used and mistreated, nor could she see that she might be to blame for the situation. As is often the case, she blamed her rival for her problems.

A Broken Date leads to a Fight and a Death

The fight between Wade and Ludemann exploded into the real world when Camacho sent Wade a text message saying he would see her.

He then sent another text message breaking off the date. Wade suspected that Camacho had broken off the date so he could see Ludemann.

For some reason, this angered Ludemann and caused her to pick up a knife and head over to the apartment where Rachel was staying. Wade fled to a friend's house, but Ludemann tracked her there. Ludemann was reportedly driving so fast that she almost tipped her minivan over as she sped towards the house.

When she saw her rival pull up outside, Rachel Wade apparently snapped. She grabbed a kitchen knife and headed out to Ludemann's van. As she approached the van, Ludemann jumped on her, but was stabbed with the knife. When police arrived, Wade was calmly smoking a cigarette as Ludemann bled to death on the ground nearby. She reportedly asked police for another cigarette when they arrived.

Death by Stabbing

The murder scene was made more dramatic by the presence of Sarah Ludemann's parents. Ludemann's father reportedly called Wade names as the police arrived and arrested her.

Rachel Wade was eventually convicted of second degree murder despite testimony that Sarah Ludemann was the aggressor. Since both girls were the aggressors, it's easy to see why the jury ignored this defense. Interestingly enough, it was a collection of threatening voicemail messages that Rachel Wade had sent to Sarah that convinced the jury she was capable of deliberate murder.

At the trial in 2009, prosecutors described a particularly violent attack by Wade. They noted that Wade had been attacked with such force that the blade of the knife she used had been bent. The voicemail messages played in court were so violent and shocking that they silenced the jury.

Social Media and Love Triangles don't Mix

The death of Sarah Ludemann proves that social media and love triangles don't mix. Rachel Wade apparently found out about the affair when pictures of Ludemann and Camacho were posted on her MySpace page. There was no way that privacy could be maintained in the virtual world of cyberspace. There are no secrets in social media, especially for cheating lovers.

Rachel Wade was eventually sentenced to 27 years in prison for stabbing Sarah Ludemann to death. She'll spend most of her adult life behind bars if she serves the entire sentence. In an interview she gave on the ABC television show 20/20, Wade said she is now sorry and even apologized to Ludemann's parents. She also said that she now wishes she had sat down with Ludemann and worked things out.

Unfortunately, she didn't think of that at the time of the murder. Persons who commit crimes of passion rarely do. They act rather than think and suffer terrible consequences.

Bibliography

Dorian, Marc. "Teenage Love Triangle Turns Deadly." 18 November 2010. abcnews.go.com . 20/20 News Article . 24 February 2013.

Hayes, Kevin. "Rachel Wade Guilty of Sarah Ludemman Murder: Teenage Love Triangle Verdict." 23 July 2010. cbsnews.com . CBS News Article . 24 February 2013.

—. "Rachel Wade Sentenced: Teenage Love Triangle Murderer Gets 27 years for Death of Sarah Ludemann." 3 September 2010. cbsnews.com . CBS News Article . 24 February 2013.

Huff, Steve. "The Saga of Rachel Wade and Sarah Ludemann." 15 April 2009. truecrimereport.com . True Crime Report Article . 24 February 2013.

Dr. Louis Chen: Surgeon, Father and Murderer

Crimes of passion are equal opportunity offenses. They cross all racial, sexual, class, and economic boundaries. All lovers, including gay lovers, are capable of slaughtering their partners in a fit of rage. Any sort of love can turn to hatred and violence in a short period of time and lead to crimes.

A perfect example of the universality of crimes of passion is Dr. Louis Chen of Seattle. Chen, a doctor, stabbed his lover, Eric Cooper, and his two-year-old son to death in a fit of rage on Aug. 11, 2011. Dr. Chen's story is made all the more chilling by the fact that he and Cooper had gone to great lengths to have a son.

A Horrific Discovery

The people of Seattle became aware of Dr. Louis Chen on the morning of Aug. 11, 2011, when a nurse from Virginia Mason Medical Center came to see why Chen hadn't reported for work. Chen was working in the Center's Endocrinology Department.

When the nurse, Madonna Carlson, came to Chen's penthouse apartment, she discovered a scene of horror. Chen was naked and covered with blood when she opened the door, and Cooper's body could be seen lying on the living room floor. Carlson called 911, and officers were dispatched. The police discovered Louis Chen's son, Cooper, lying dead on the bathroom floor. They also discovered two more kitchen knives covered with blood. Chen, who had a black eye, told the police he had committed the crime and surrendered to them.

An examination of the crime scene produced evidence of an intensely savage crime.

Eric Cooper had been stabbed at least 100 times, and at least one of the stabbings had been done with such force that it broke the knife. Chen himself had several knife wounds on his body, which indicated that he had stabbed himself during the crime.

Passion Leads to Family and Murder

Frighteningly enough, the relationship of Dr. Louis Chen and Eric Cooper had been a passionate one. Yet there is also evidence that Chen was obsessed with Cooper to the point of insanity.

Eric Cooper was a small-town boy from Tinley Park, Ill. who ran away from home to be with Dr. Chen. Chen was a Taiwanese immigrant who was studying medicine in Chicago when the two met. There's no indication of how or where the two met, but they were together for at least 11 years. Relatives said Cooper was apparently head over heels in love with Chen.

Cooper followed Chen around the country and apparently kept house for him. Chen completed his residency in internal medicine in San Diego before moving to Seattle. After completing his medical degree in Seattle, Chen worked at a VA hospital in Minneapolis and completed a clinical fellowship in endocrinology at Duke University in North Carolina. Even though Chen was well-educated, Cooper wasn't. He was a high school dropout who was working on his GED.

At some point, the two decided they wanted to have a child and went to some lengths to have one. A surrogate mother in Taiwan was reportedly impregnated with Chen's sperm. The mother gave birth to a boy named Cooper Chen, whom they brought home to America to raise. Eric stayed home to care for the baby while Louis concentrated on his medical career.

Obsession Leads to Murder

It isn't clear what turned Louis Chen from healer into savage killing machine, but obsession seems to be the key. Like many lovers who commit crimes of passion, Chen was obsessed with his partner to the point of insanity. He may have wanted to completely control and dominate Eric Cooper.

News reports indicate that Eric Cooper was thinking of breaking away from Chen in the months leading up to the murder. Cooper was reportedly working on his GED and thinking of going to college and studying nursing.

Perhaps Chen resented the independence. Whatever the cause, Louis Chen seemed to snap completely and destroy the family he had worked so hard to have. He killed both his son and his partner in the bloodiest manner possible.

Facing the Death Penalty

Dr. Louis Chen was charged with two counts of aggravated murder in the first degree. That means that he is eligible for the death penalty in Washington State. Incredibly, Chen has pleaded not guilty to the crime, even though he has confessed to it.

Chen's trial has been postponed to the summer of 2013 because there is so much evidence for attorneys to go through. Chen has also undergone an evaluation for mental competency and seems to be going for an insanity defense.

Bibliography

Cartier, Curtis. "Comment of the Week: Louis Chen Story is Being Covered up Because Not Straight and White ." 2 September 2011. seattleweekly.com. Seattle Weekly Commentary . 21 February 2013.

Clarridge, Christine. "Doctor charged in Seattle murders of partner, child ." 16 August 2011. newsobserver.com . Seattle Times Newspaper Article . 21 February 2013.

Craig, M. "Portrait of a Sociopath." 2009. sociopathworld.com. Molecular Psychology journal article reprinted at Sociopath World website. 19 February 2013.

Hamilton, Keegan. "Dr. Louis Chen Arraigned Today: Will Face Death Penalty for Brutal First Hill Murders?" 29 August 2011. seattleweekly.com. Seattle Weekly News Blog. 21 February 2013.

—. "Louis Chen Trial Postponed While State Tests Evidence from Particularly Bloody Crime Scene ." 30 March 2012. seattleweekly.com . Seattle Weekly Newspaper Article . 21 February 2013.

SociopathWorld . "Do sociopaths love?" 26 January 2009. sociopathworld.com . Blog Entry . 19 February 2013.

He Gunned Down His Wife's Teenaged Lover: Eric McLean

Love triangles often lead to crimes of passion and the death of one of the people involved. Yet few love triangles have been stranger than the one between Sean Powell, Eric McLean, and Erin McLean. Sean Powell was one of Erin's students at a high school where she was undergoing a teaching internship.

At some point, Erin McLean fell in love with Powell, moved out of the home she shared with her husband and two children, and moved in with Powell. The affair unsettled and unnerved Eric McLean, who went to the home where Powell and his wife were living. There, Eric pointed a shotgun at Powell to threaten him, but the weapon went off and Powell was killed.

The case is made all the more bizarre by the fact that Eric McLean only served 47 days in jail for killing his wife's lover. Strangely enough, the jury decided that the death was an accident and let Eric McLean walk out of the courthouse. Eric was even able to win custody of his two sons.

Devotion or Obsession: Eric and Erin McLean

Eric McLean certainly fits the profile of a certain class of people who commit crimes of passion. Like many who kill their partners or partners' lovers, Eric McLean sacrificed a great deal for the woman he loved, yet found himself abandoned for another lover.

Eric McLean had apparently given up his passion of playing with rock bands to become a high school band director, probably so he could be with his wife. He then put his academic career at the University of Tennessee on hold and delivered pizzas to support his wife and children. Even though Eric left school, Erin stayed to complete her master's degree and advance her own career.

A Shotgun Killer Gets Away with It

The tragic love triangle came to a head in March 2007, when Eric McLean decided to confront Sean Powell outside his home. McLean took a loaded shotgun to the confrontation, which indicates he was planning to murder Powell. The shotgun was also apparently loaded with ammunition heavy enough to kill a human being, another sign of premeditated murder.

The confrontation fell apart, and McLean eventually fired on Powell at close range and killed him. McLean's claim was that he was simply trying to scare Powell away, but a more likely scenario is that he deliberately set out to gun down the young man.

After the killing, McLean fled and was eventually found walking along some railroad tracks outside the city of Knoxville, Tenn. He was still carrying the shotgun when police caught up with him, and he surrendered without incident. That might indicate Eric was planning suicide, but decided against it.

The Runaway Wife and the Killer who got Away with it

The case took more bizarre turns. Eric McLean was convicted of reckless homicide, a low level felony under Tennessee law. He only served a minimum sentence of 47 days in jail and walked free.

Erin McLean, meanwhile, disappeared from sight. She had fled and taken her two young sons with her. Authorities eventually found Erin living in Austin, Texas with another 18-year-old man. Erin described the man as her "helper", but Eric described him as Erin's new boyfriend. Erin was arrested and extradited to Tennessee.

A judge in Texas then awarded temporary custody of the boys to Eric's mother.

Once there, she actually faced a longer jail sentence than Eric had, 90 days behind bars. The threat of jail prompted Erin to back down and make an agreement with Eric. She gave up custody of the boys in exchange for her freedom.

Erin McLean Got a Young Man Killed and Destroyed Her Own Life

Part of the reason why the jury may have went easy on Eric is that they felt sorry for him. Court testimony indicated that Erin had been flaunting the affair and rubbing it in, as sociopaths often do. She had an idea of the effect her behavior might have on her husband.

Nor did she seem to realize that an affair with an 18-year-old boy would end her teaching career. She lost her job at West High School in Knoxville and probably her chance to teach again. In other words, everything that Erin had studied so hard to achieve in college was lost. Her master's degree was now useless.

Since the shooting, Eric McLean has been living in Knoxville and raising his two sons. Erin McLean has dropped out of sight, although media reports indicate that she moved back to Austin. It is not known whether she is living with another 18-year-old again or not.

Bibliography

Associated Press . "Affair Between Student and Married Teacher Leads to Teen's Murder in Tennessee ." 18 March 2007. foxnews.com. Wire Service News Article . 24 February 2013.

—. "Tennessee Teacher Living With New Teen Lover After Sex Slaying Case." 2 October 2008. foxnews.com. Wire Service News Article . 24 February 2013.

Craig, M. "Portrait of a Sociopath." 2009. sociopathworld.com. Molecular Psychology journal article reprinted at Sociopath World website. 19 February 2013.

Mcaffee.cc. "Profile of the Sociopath." n.d. mcafee.cc . Online Database Entry. 15 February 2013.

Satterfield, Jamie. "Eric McLean gets 47 days in death." 8 November 2008.

knoxnews.com . Knoxville News Sentinel
Newspaper Article . 24 February 2013.

—. "Eric McLean wins custody battle over
sons." 19 February 2009. knoxnews.com.
Knoxville News Sentinel newspaper article . 24
February 2013.

SociopathWorld . "Do sociopaths love?" 26
January 2009. sociopathworld.com . Blog Entry
. 19 February 2013.

LISA NOWAK: KILLER ASTRONAUT IN DIAPERS

Nobody is immune to mental illness and the crimes of passion it can produce, not even the most highly educated and experienced professionals. Nothing proves this more than the case of Lisa Nowak, an astronaut and U.S. Navy captain who stalked and tried to kidnap a romantic rival.

Nowak got caught up in a bizarre love triangle that led to tragedy and created a media circus. The case attracted attention because a person who is supposed to be sane and disciplined acted in the most violent and bizarre manner possible. Ironically enough, the case attracted a lot of attention because of a piece of Nowak's alleged wardrobe: adult diapers.

She Drove 900 Miles to Attack a Rival

The drama began at Orlando International Airport in February 2007 when somebody tried to incapacitate Air Force captain Colleen Shipman with pepper spray in a parking lot. The crime was particularly baffling because surveillance cameras showed the attacker was a woman wearing a disguise right out of a comic book: a trench coat and a wig.

The attack was clumsy and quickly failed. Shipman was never affected by the pepper spray and managed to get away. Police arrived at the scene and found a duffle bag containing a BB pistol, a two-pound mallet, and surgical tubing. From this, they inferred that Nowak was planning to knock Shipman out and tie her up. What she was planning to do with her victim after the attack is still unknown. Detectives were able to track Nowak down with evidence from the car.

When police made an arrest, two details quickly caught the public's attention about the identity of the attacker: She was an astronaut and she wore adult diapers. Police found adult diapers in Nowak's car; from this, they inferred she had driven all the way from her home in Houston to Orlando, a distance of 900 miles, and crossed five states without stopping. The presence of diapers isn't unusual; astronauts wear diapers when leaving and entering space because they can't take a bathroom break during liftoff and reentry.

An Affair Leads to Self-Destruction

Lisa Nowak hardly fits the profile of an obsessed woman who turns to crime. She is a graduate of the U.S. Naval Academy. She is also a Navy pilot and an astronaut who held a master's degree in aeronautical engineering. In addition to being an astronaut, Nowak had been a test pilot for the Navy. Nowak had at least one mission on the space shuttle Discovery that lasted 13 days in 2006.

In her personal life, Nowak was something of an overachiever; she had three children and claimed to be a gourmet cook. Other hobbies included playing the piano, running, skeet shooting, sailing, and playing the piano. Yet all of that fell apart when she met another astronaut named William Oefelein.

After a short affair with Oefelein, Nowak seemed to snap and started planning her attack on Shipman. Ironically enough, Nowak was married to the father of her children, Robert T. Nowak, at the time of the attack.

Disgrace and a Successful Defense

Nowak was able to get off with only a year of probation because of a legal technicality. Yet she saw her life completely destroyed; she was dismissed from the astronaut corps and dishonorably discharged from the Navy. She was also stripped of the rank of captain shortly before her discharge. Nowak's husband divorced her around the time of the incident.

So why did Lisa Nowak do what she did? Why did she destroy her life for a man she barely knew? The answer seems to lie in her psychology, or rather in a personality disorder. Her behavior seems to indicate an obsessive compulsive personality disorder. Nowak's lawyer was prepared to use that as defense at her trial and introduce evidence of other problems, including a bipolar disorder and Asperger's syndrome. Some psychologists have noted that Nowak doesn't meet the criteria for these conditions.

Such disorders often lead to crimes of passion because people with one can become obsessed with a particular individual. The obsession becomes irrational and compels them to behave in an unusual or outrageous manner.

High Functioning Persons and Personality Disorders

This hypothesis seems to fly in conventional wisdom; after all, Lisa Nowak had a successful career, family life, and marriage. She was able to function normally in society for years. The Nowak case indicates that persons with such disorders can function normally or at least appear to do so.

Whether Lisa Nowak can rebuild her life remains unclear. She has dropped out of sight since the attack on Shipman, who now claims to have post-traumatic stress disorder as a result of her run-in with Nowak.

The case of Lisa Nowak should give all of us pause; even the most successful and attractive individuals might be harboring bizarre personality disorders that could lead to a crime of passion. Everybody should keep that in mind when they date or start looking for a prospective spouse.

Bibliography

A.D.A.M. Encyclopedia . "Obsessive-compulsive disorder." 7 March 2012. www.ncbi.nlm.nih.gov. Online Database Entry . 20 February 2013.

Associated Press. "Ex-Astronaut Lisa Nowak Forced Out of Navy." 29 July 2011. foxnews.com . Wire Service News Article . 20 February 2013.

Greene, Nick. "Lisa Nowak." n.d. space.about.com. Profile at About.com . 20 February 2013.

Strauss, Eric M. "Did Astronaut Lisa Nowak, Love Triangle Attacker, Wear Diaper." 17 February 2011. abcnews.go.com . ABC 20/20 News Feature. 20 February 2013.

Vox, Ford. "Lisa Nowak: Space Oddity." 17 February 2011. theatlantic.com . Atlantic Magazine Column. 20 February 2013.

Wikipedia. "Lisa Nowak." n.d. en.wikipedia.org. Online Encyclopedia Entry. 20 February 2013.

PIERRE AND YVONNE CHEVALLIER: MISMATCHED MARRIAGE LEADS TO MURDER

Even though the idea of opposites attracting is a popular romantic notion, it can have very bad results and sometimes lead to crimes of passion. When different people with different personalities and lifestyles try to make a romance work, the results are often explosive.

This is clearly shown in the case of Pierre Chevallier, a French doctor, war hero, and rising political figure who was shot by his wife.

The Chevallier case was one of the most followed in French history because it involved a well-known politician. It led to one of the most followed trials of the 20th century and a classic example of the media circus that often develops around sensational crimes. The interesting thing is that the whole crime began as a mismatched love affair.

The Ugly Duckling and the Suave Doctor

Pierre Chevallier and his wife, Yvonne, were certainly opposites. Chevallier was a handsome, highly intelligent, and debonair medical student when he married Yvonne in 1935 in Orleans, France. Yvonne was dull and homely and comfortable in the role of housewife and mother. She was also sort of frumpy and definitely socially inept.

The differences became a problem as the two moved on. Chevallier became a doctor, and then during World War II, a leader of the

French resistance against the Nazis. He was a natural leader and soon rose to a high position in the underground in Orleans. Pierre was also a very brave man; he faced torture and murder at the hands of the Gestapo if the Nazis ever caught him. For his wartime exploits, Pierre received two of France's best-known medals, the Legion d'Honneur (Legion of Honor) and Croix de Guerre.

After the war, Pierre threw himself into politics and was elected the mayor of Orleans. The couple started travelling to Paris, where Pierre had been asked to participate in the national government. He was asked to join the cabinet by 1950.

A Rising Politician and an Affair

The glittering and sophisticated social life in post-war Paris highlighted the differences between the two. It also displayed Yvonne's inadequacies for all to see. Pierre was cultured and well-read and accepted in high society, but Yvonne was not.

Pierre began pressing her to change her appearance and manners because it was clear she was becoming a hindrance to his political ambitions. Yvonne tried to change, but failed. She was still homely and frumpy. Like many successful men on the rise, Pierre began looking for a new and more glamorous wife.

An Anonymous Letter Leads to Murder

In 1951, Yvonne received an anonymous letter that said her husband was having an affair. The letter prompted Yvonne to search her husband's pockets, and she found a letter that was signed Jeannette. Yvonne figured that "Jeannette" was Jeanne Perreau, her beautiful, sophisticated, and highly intelligent neighbor in Orleans. Jeanne was also married to Orleans' richest hotel owner.

When Yvonne confronted Pierre about the affair, he simply ignored her and treated her with contempt. This caused Yvonne to snap, and she tried to commit suicide in an effort to attract Pierre's attention. When that failed, she obtained a handgun permit and purchased a semiautomatic pistol.

Shortly afterwards, Pierre was appointed France's Minister of Education. Pierre then completely dismissed Yvonne and announced plans to marry his trophy wife. Yvonne confronted Pierre and threatened to commit suicide. He simply told her to do it, but instead, she fired five rounds at her husband. One of them hit the mark and killed him.

A Sensational Murder and a Media Sensation

In a disturbing development, Pierre's body was found by his 11-year-old son, Mathieu. The boy also saw his mother standing over his father's body, holding a gun. Yvonne went downstairs, called the police, and asked Gendarmes to come over because her husband needed help.

Not surprisingly, the trial created a media sensation because Pierre Chevallier had just been appointed Minister of Education. The trial would quickly degenerate into a media circus and a soap opera.

Yvonne Chevallier's trial attracted the attention of the world's media. Major American and British newspapers and magazines sent reporters. All of France's attention was glued up on the Palace of Justice in Reims where the trial was held.

She got off because her Husband was having an Affair

Yvonne Chevallier escaped prison and the guillotine because of a bizarre clause in the French penal code. When she was tried in 1952, a killing was not a homicide under French law if a husband killed a wife who was a having an affair. There is even a French term for such an incident, "Crime Passionnel," which translates to crime of passion in English. Yvonne's lawyers argued that a woman should enjoy the same questionable "right."

Crowds of protestors, mostly women, gathered outside the courthouse and began protesting on behalf of Yvonne. The case was caught up in French politics; France was behind the rest of Europe because women had not been given the right to vote until after World War II. French society was notoriously sexist and women were definitely second class citizens. The dumpy housewife Yvonne Chevallier had unwittingly become a symbol of women's rights in France.

The protestors added to the media circus, which was enlivened when both Jeanne Perreau and her husband were called to testify. Perreau testified that an affair had occurred. The presiding judge then lectured Yvonne on her animal passion and turned the case over to the jury. The all-male jury deliberated for 45 minutes and declared Yvonne not guilty. They agreed that French people had the right to kill unfaithful spouses.

Yvonne Chevallier walked free to the cheers of the crowd. She then moved to French New Guinea, where she served as a volunteer nurse at a hospital for the poor until her death in the 1970s. She had gotten away with murder and struck a strange blow for sexual equality.

The Psychological Dangers of Mismatched Romance

Mismatched romances, particularly those that cross class or racial lines or involve people with completely different personalities, often lead to crimes of passion. Part of the reason for this is that one partner often lives his or her fantasies through the other and finds fulfillment that way. This seems to be the case with Yvonne Chevallier. She lived for her husband and needed him to make her complete.

Yvonne Chevallier was a passionate woman, but Pierre Chevallier was a user. A cold and calculating individual who chose his women for what they could do for him. When he was a struggling medical student, he needed a supportive wife like Yvonne. As a politician, he needed a glamorous hostess like Jeanne Perreau.

Bibliography

Craig, M. "Portrait of a Sociopath." 2009. sociopathworld.com. Molecular Psychology journal article reprinted at Sociopath World website. 19 February 2013.

Krajicek, David. "Crime Passionel ." n.d. trutv.com/library/crime . Online Encyclopedia Entry . 24 February 2013.

Mcaffee.cc. "Profile of the Sociopath." n.d. mcafee.cc . Online Database Entry. 15 February 2013.

MURDER REVISTED . "YVONNE CHEVAL-LIER - CRIME PASSIONEL." 13 August 2009. murderrevisited.blogspot.com . Blog Entry. 24 February 2013.

SociopathWorld . "Do sociopaths love?" 26 January 2009. sociopathworld.com . Blog Entry . 19 February 2013.

SHE KILLED HER OWN DAUGHTER FOR LOVE: DENISE LABBE

Most crimes of passion involve the killing of a lover or a romantic rival, but the crime committed by Frenchwoman Denise Labbe is particularly chilling and horrific. She killed her own two-year-old daughter in order to please a man she loved.

The lover was Jacques Algarron, who was a devotee of the brilliant but deranged German philosopher Friedrich Nietzsche. Algarron, who was supposedly a philosophy student, believed that reading Nietzsche had turned him into a superman. How this justified the killing of a child is hard to determine. Nietzsche's works say nothing about the killing of children.

Algarron basically told Labbe that she had to murder her daughter Catherine in order to prove her love to him. The frightening thing is that she apparently loved Algarron so much that she was willing to kill her child for him. Worse, she made at least three attempts on Catherine's life.

From Lonely Orphan to Cold-Blooded Killer

Part of the reason for Labbe's behavior might be found in her background. She was a lonely young woman living in France in the early 1950s. She had reportedly been orphaned at the age of 13, and since that would have been in 1944, there is a strong possibility that her parents were killed in World War II or murdered by the Nazis, who were then occupying

France. Labbe had to start supporting herself in menial jobs, such as a hotel maid.

The adoration from Algarron might have filled a need in her lonely life. He was a college student and younger than her. She might have found him as her only ticket to a better life and only chance for love. This sounds disturbing, like an obsessive compulsive disorder.

The love affair led to murder in November 1954, when the two were living in Rennes, France. Algarron had been becoming more and more demanding. He had also become obsessed with the idea that Labbe must prove her love by murdering Catherine. He threatened to leave her unless she killed the toddler.

She Made Four Attempts on Her Daughter's Life

Denise Labbe made three attempts to carry out Algarron's wishes before finally succeeding. She tried dropping the child out of a window, but couldn't go through with the plan. Next, Denise threw Catherine into a canal, but a passerby saw the incident and saved the little girl.

Finally, Denise drowned Catherine in a wash tub in her own home. The woman actually held her daughter in the water until she was dead. She killed her daughter with her own hands in the name of love.

As what often happens in such incidents, the police soon discovered the horror and arrested both Denise and Jacques. Instead of spending their lives together, the two got to spend a very long time in French prisons, which were then some of the most barbaric in Europe. Denise was sentenced to life and Jacques to 20 years of hard labor.

Why Did They Do it?

What could possess a mother to kill her own child, and what hold could a man have over her to make her do such a thing? More importantly, why did Jacques Algarron behave in the way that he did?

On some level, the killing might have been an "experiment" by Algarron to see what he could make another human being do for him. Thankfully, he was arrested and imprisoned before he could commit any other such experiments.

Is Nietzsche to Blame?

Like many sociopaths, Algarron was obsessed with Nietzsche's idea of the superman. The superman is a highly intelligent and capable being that can transcend normal morality. Algarron apparently thought he was the superman, or he could become one.

Nietzsche has inspired other crimes, such as Nathan F. Leopold Jr. and Richard Albert Loeb, two Chicago teenagers who kidnapped a 14-year-old boy named Robert Franks and murdered him for a thrill in 1924. Some people believe that Nietzsche's ideas may have inspired the Nazis.

Yet blaming Nietzsche for Algarron's behavior is a stretch. In reality, it was the philosophy student's own personality flaws that drove him to manipulate his lover into murdering her child.

How Sociopaths Use Love to Destroy

This case shows why sociopaths are so dangerous; even love can be a tool of control and a weapon of destruction in their hands. Since they are incapable of empathy and ethical behaviors, sociopaths simply see love as a tool to use to get what they want. That means they can engineer crimes of passion to appease their own twisted desires.

Bibliography

Buckle, Nickey. "Denise Labbe." n.d. murderpedia.org. Online Encyclopedia Entry. 21 February 2013.

Craig, M. "Portrait of a Sociopath." 2009. sociopathworld.com. Molecular Psychology journal article reprinted at Sociopath World website. 19 February 2013.

Davison-Forder, Jania. "Crime of Passion - Where Emotions are deadly!" n.d. murderpedia.org . Article Reprinted at murperpedia.org . 21 February 2013.

Mcaffee.cc. "Profile of the Sociopath." n.d. mcafee.cc . Online Database Entry. 15 February 2013.

Rackcliffee, M. "LeopoldandLoeb.com." 2013. leopoldandloeb.com. Website dedicated to Leopold and Loeb. 21 February 2013.

SociopathWorld . "Do sociopaths love?" 26 January 2009. sociopathworld.com . Blog Entry . 19 February 2013.

Time Magazine. "France: the Possessed." 11 June 1956. Time.com/time/magazine/archive. Time Magazine article from 1956 in online archive. 21 February 2013.

She Was Shot by the Long Island Lolita: Mary Jo Buttafuoco

The Sordid Affair that Became a Media Sensation

In 1992, a sordid affair between a troubled teenager and a local auto body shop owner in a Long Island suburb became a media sensation. The affair generated a media circus of almost mythic proportions because it prompted a 16-year-old girl to shoot her married lover's wife.

The media became aware of Amy Fisher, the young girl soon to be immortalized as the Long Island Lolita, when she went to the door of the Buttafuoco house in Merrick, NY. After she rang the doorbell and waited as the lady of the house, Mary Jo Buttafuoco, came to the door, Fisher shot her in the head.

The brutal murder attempt would launch all three people involved into long careers as B-list celebrities. It would also turn a questionable relationship into the kind of media sensation that marked the 1990s.

Lolita and the Married Mechanic

The reasons for the shooting are not clear, but they probably involve 16-year-old Amy Fisher's obsession with Joey Buttafuoco. The two had started an affair about a year earlier in his shop. At the time of the affair, Fisher was reportedly working as a prostitute through an escort agency.

The trouble began when Fisher asked Buttafuoco to leave his wife and marry her. When she refused, Amy apparently concocted the plan to shoot Mary Jo. Some reports indicate that Fisher had also been trying to shake Joey down for money, but he refused.

Fisher's execution of the crime was neither very sophisticated nor smart. She let Mary Jo Buttafuoco see her and wore a t-shirt from Joey's auto body shop that was easy to identify. If that wasn't clumsy enough, Fisher didn't bother to finish the job by firing a few more rounds into Mary Jo's head. Mary Jo not only lived, but she was also able to tell the police who was behind the attack.

The Media Circus Begins

Many people will wonder why the Buttafuoco case attracted so much attention. The most likely reason is that it occurred on Long Island, just a short drive from New York City, America's media capitol. Another reason is that New York is the only major American city that still has a tabloid press devoted to such scandals. In most U.S. cities, newspapers are fairly stodgy and conservative and leave sensational stories to TV stations. Plus, the case broke just as tabloid television was becoming popular in the U.S. It made perfect fodder for such shows.

Joey and Amy Get Convicted

Both Joey Buttafuoco and Amy Fisher would ultimately face criminal charges over the incident. Buttafuoco pleaded guilty to statutory rape (having sex with a minor) and served four months in jail because of the affair.

Amy Fisher pleaded guilty to aggravated assault in December 1992 and was sentenced to 15 years in prison. Fisher was released from prison under a new plea agreement based on Mary Jo's wishes in 1995. Fisher later claimed to have been raped by a guard while in prison, but presented no evidence of it.

Everybody Becomes a Celebrity

All three members of the love triangle ultimately cashed in on their newfound fame by becoming B-list celebrities. Joey Buttafuoco became an actor and appeared in such dubious public events as the 2006 Lingerie Bowl and on the notorious reality TV show Celebrity Boxing.

There, his claim to fame was giving another notorious celebrity, Tanya Harding, a vicious thrashing. Buttafuoco is currently starring in B movies such as Gangsta Mafia. He was also convicted of insurance fraud while living in California.

Incredibly, the Buttafuocos stayed together for 11 years and even moved across the country to Ventura County, Calif. so Joey could pursue his "career" in Hollywood. Mary Jo divorced Joey in 2003, and her appearance, which had been destroyed by Mary Fisher's bullets, was restored by plastic surgery a few years later.

Mary Jo wrote a book with the ponderous title of Getting It Through My Thick Skull: Why I Stayed, What I Learned, and What Millions of People Involved with Sociopaths Need to Know. As the book's title implies, Mary Jo now considers Joey Buttafuoco a sociopath, which is defined as a charming and manipulative person with no regard for others and who ignores normal moral standards.

Amy Fisher Today

Amy Fisher left prison in 1999 and became a successful journalist, writing columns for The Long Island Press. The former Lolita wrote a book, married, had two children, and became as sleazy as Joey Buttafuoco in her attempts to cash in. In 2009, she even made a pornographic film called Amy Fisher: Totally Nude and Exposed. She also sold sex tapes to porn distributors.

The Long Island Lolita case proves that the urge for the fast buck is stronger than the emotions that generate crimes of passion. It also shows that Amy Fisher may also be a sociopath.

Bibliography

Adams, Mike. "How to Spot a Sociopath ." 8 June 2012. naturalnews.com . Online News Article . 19 February 2013.

Bio True Story. "Amy Fisher Biography." n.d. biography.com . Synopsis of Amy Fisher's Life . 17 February 2013.

Buttafuoco, Mary Jo. "Mary Jo Buttfafuouco Author and Keynote Speaker ." n.d. maryjo-buttafuocuo.co . Mary Jo Buttaffuoco official website. 19 February 2013.

Contact Music . "Buttafuoco to Play Mafia Boss ." 30 June 2003. contactmusic.com . News Article . 19 February 2013.

Wikipedia . "Joey Buttafuoco ." n.d. en.wikipedia.org. Online Encyclopedia Entry . 19 February 2013.

—. "Lolita ." n.d. en.wikipedia.org. Online Encyclopedia Entry . 19 February 2013.

—. "Mary Jo Buttafuoco ." n.d. en.wikipedia.org. Online Encyclopedia Entry. 19 February 2013.

FROM ALL-AMERICAN TO CRIME OF PASSION VICTIM: STEVE MCNAIR

Death of a Quarterback

Even celebrities and sports heroes can become victims of love and passion turned to rage and hatred. A chilling example of such a crime was the murder that claimed the life of famed NFL quarterback Steve McNair.

On July 4, 2009, the people of Nashville, Tenn. were shocked by the bizarre death of one of their hometown heroes, former Tennessee Titans and Baltimore Ravens quarterback Steve McNair. McNair, who had retired a little over a year earlier, was a well-known figure around Nashville.

The former quarterback had been shot several times in a condominium in downtown Nashville on Independence Day. The body of his mistress, Sahel Kazemi, a local waitress, was found in the condominium. Kazemi had apparently shot herself after pumping a large number of bullets into McNair. The number of bullets fired suggests that a great deal of rage was involved in the crime.

"Air McNair" and the Mystery Woman

There is a great deal of mystery involved in Steve McNair's shooting. The motive for the crime is still unknown, and little is known about Sahel Kazemi. What is known is that she and McNair were having an affair and he had apparently given her large amounts of money. She was working as a waitress, yet she was driving a two-year-old Cadillac Escalade at the time of her death.

The only details available about Kazemi's background were that she was from Iran, she was an orphan, and she was raised by an aunt in Florida. Media accounts indicate that her parents were both killed in Iran because they had run afoul of that nation's oppressive government.

McNair apparently kept his relationship with Kazemi a closely-guarded secret. Media accounts indicate that neither his wife nor his older brother knew about the affair, even though he was apparently giving Kazemi money. He may have also arranged to get her a waitress job at Opry Mills, a restaurant where he liked to hang out.

A Self-Made Football Star

In contrast to Sahel Kazemi, Steve McNair's life was an open book. He was a rare self-made NFL star who had taken an unorthodox route to football's big show. McNair had grown up in Mississippi and became known as Air McNair for his high school football prowess. He turned down a full scholarship to the University of Florida in order to play the position he wanted, quarterback, at the obscure Alcorn State University.

McNair was able to rise to become the third overall draft pick in the 1995 NFL draft. He was the highest drafted African-American quarterback in NFL history when the Houston Oilers signed him. When the Oilers moved to Tennessee and became the Titans, McNair became their quarterback. On Jan. 30, 2000, he and the Titans faced the St. Louis Rams in Super Bowl XXXIV, where the Rams defeated the Titans, 23-16. In 2006, McNair was traded to the Baltimore Ravens for a fourth-round draft pick, but by then, his career was fading because of injuries. The injuries eventually ended his playing days in 2008.

Infidelity Leads to Tragedy and Death

Steven McNair and his wife, Mechelle, had two sons, but reports indicate that he had two other sons by other women, which indicates infidelity was nothing new with him. Media reports indicate that Mechelle McNair was unaware of the relationship between Steve and Kazemi.

Other reports indicate that Kazemi believed that McNair was planning to divorce his wife and marry her. Whether he was lying to her or she was simply delusional is unknown. One strong possibility is that Kazemi discovered that McNair was not planning to divorce his wife, which prompted her to shoot him.

Another is that McNair had decided to break off the affair because it had been discovered. On July 2, 2009, Nashville police had pulled over a 2007 Cadillac Escalade because its driver appeared to be drunk. The driver was Kazemi, and the passengers were McNair and an employee at his restaurant, Vent Gordon. Police allowed McNair and Gordon to leave in a taxi, but arrested and jailed Kazemi.

Like many star athletes, McNair apparently got preferential treatment from the police. This might have enraged Kazemi, who reportedly bought a gun on the black market from a convicted murderer after the incident. That gun was used to murder Steve McNair.

Bibliography

Craig, M. "Portrait of a Sociopath." 2009. sociopathworld.com. Molecular Psychology journal article reprinted at Sociopath World website. 19 February 2013.

Ghianni, Tim. "Steve McNair's wife was unaware of affair with Sahel Kazemi until husband's death." 6 July 2009. dailynews.com/sports. NY Daily News newspaper article . 17 February 2013.

Hall, Kristin M. "Steve McNair Dead." 5 July 2009. huffingtonpost.com. Associated Press Wire Service News Article . 19 February 2013.

Howard, Kate. "Steve McNair and Sahel Kazemi killed ." 4 July 2009. tennessean.com . Tennessean newspaper article . 19 February 2013.

SociopathWorld . "Do sociopaths love?" 26 January 2009. sociopathworld.com . Blog Entry . 19 February 2013.

Wikipedia . "Steve McNair." n.d. en.wikipedia.org. Online Encyclopedia Entry. 19 February 2013.

THE HOLLYWOOD DREAM BECOMES A NIGHTMARE: THE MURDER OF PHIL HARTMAN

An Unusual Murder Suicide

Murder suicides involving married couples usually follow a certain pattern. The husband kills the wife, then kills himself. Such violence often occurs with poor couples facing economic hardships. That makes the murder of legendary comic Phil Hartman by his wife very unusual.

At the time of the murder, Hartman and his wife, Brynn, were enjoying the heights of success. Phil Hartman was starring in a successful primetime sitcom, and the couple and their children lived in a $1.4 million mansion in Encino, Calif. Friends and coworkers described them as happy and always together. So it's not surprising that America was shocked when Brynn Hartman shot her husband in the head, then turned the gun on herself. The case seems to defy logic and popular stereotypes.

The Hollywood Dream becomes a Nightmare

In 1998, Phil and Brynn Hartman were apparently living the Hollywood dream. Brynn Hartman was a small town girl from Thief River Falls, Minn. who had become a model in California and married one of America's most popular comedians. Hartman was an over-the-top performer who had found big success as a comedian and later a comic character actor.

The couple's dream life, in a large house in Encino, Calif., was actually a charade. The Hartmans' fame and fortune masked serious marital discord and mental health problems. Like many performers, the Hartmans were expert at hiding their problems from even their family and friends.

Few people knew that Brynn Hartman had a longtime battle with drugs and alcohol or that Phil was emotionally distant and hard to be with. Nor did they realize that Brynn was capable of violent rages. Phil's public persona of a jovial, down-to-Earth guy was as much of an act as any of his impersonations. In private, he was emotionally distant and sometimes fought with Brynn. These secrets and more came out on the night of May 28, 1998 when Brynn Hartman shot and killed Phil before turning the gun on herself.

Did Phil Hartman's Success cause his Death?

The motive for Brynn Hartman's crime is still unknown, but jealousy might have played a role. In 1998, Phil Hartman was enjoying a wave of success; he was starring on News Radio, a sitcom on NBC, then the nation's most popular TV network, and doing voicework for the iconic cartoon show The Simpsons. Phil had also managed to win supporting roles in several A-list Hollywood movies, including Jingle All the Way.

By that time, Phil Hartman had become a TV star; he had appeared in 153 episodes of Saturday Night Live and three seasons of News Radio. His growing success took a toll on his marriage because his wife didn't share in it.

At the same time, Brynn Hartman was something of a failure; her acting career had gone nowhere and her modeling career was over. She was apparently growing restless and frustrated in her marriage with the emotionally distant Phil. Brynn Hartman also suffered from serious issues of self-esteem; she had several plastic surgeries to improve her appearance.

A Female Jekyll and Hyde

Media accounts depict Brynn Hartman as a sort of female Jekyll and Hyde. Outside the home, she projected an image as a contented wife and a confident and beautiful woman. She was also considered a wonderful mother to her young children, Sean and Birgen. Yet inside the home, Brynn Hartman was a very different person; she was insecure and regularly threw violent temper tantrums.

Brynn was also a recovering cocaine addict and alcoholic. Addiction may have played a role in the shooting, and some reports indicated that Brynn had started drinking again and Phil was unhappy about it. Phil may have threatened to divorce her if she didn't stop drinking.

The charade came apart on May 27, 1998. Brynn came home from a night of drinking and got into a fight with Phil. She apparently threw a temper tantrum which Phil Hartman simply ignored. Unable to attract his attention, Brynn took a gun out of her husband's gun safe and fired two bullets into Phil's head and one round into his chest as he slept while her children were sleeping upstairs.

She then drove to the house of her friend, Ron Douglas, and told him what she had done. Douglas didn't believe her until he followed her home and saw Phil's body. Douglas called 911 and tried to get the children to safety with the help of the police. Shortly after officers arrived, they heard a gunshot. Brynn Hartman, possibly realizing that she was about to be arrested for murder, had shot herself in the head. Her body was found lying on a bed next to Phil's lifeless corpse.

An Unusual Murder

There are many unusual aspects to Phil Hartman's murder. It fits the classic pattern of a spouse or partner who murders somebody right before a breakup, yet it was the woman and not the man who committed the murder. Like many men who murder their lovers, Brynn then killed herself.

Yet the crime might not be one of passion; the killing of Phil Hartman was definitely cold-blooded. Brynn shot him while he was asleep and deliberately aimed for his head. That indicates she might have intended to try and blame the crime on somebody else, perhaps a burglar. She might have thought Ron Douglas would help her cover up the crime, but instead, he betrayed her. She only killed herself after Ron called the police.

There is also an element of psychotic behavior involved: Brynn Hartman seemed to be out of touch with reality. Perhaps she believed she could get away with her crime and others would help her. Douglas's betrayal might have triggered Brynn's suicide.

Why did the Perfect Hollywood Wife Murder her Husband?

The question of a motive also comes up, and one possibility is that Brynn wanted to inherit all of Phil Hartman's money. Another is that she might have been afraid of losing custody of her children. She had a history of violent behavior and substance abuse, which could have been used against her in a divorce proceeding.

There is no saying what motivated Brynn, but her actions took her children far from Hollywood. They grew up in Eau Clair, Wisc., under the care of Brynn's sister.

Bibliography

CNN. "Phil Hartman, wife die in apparent murder-suicide." 28 May 1998. cnn.com/SHOWBIZ/TV. Wire Service News Article . 18 February 2013.

Moore, Solomon. "Actor Phil Hartman, Wife Killed in Murder-Suicide." 29 May 1998. articles.latimes.com/1998. Los Angeles Times Newspaper Article . 18 February 2013.

Tresniowski, Alex. "Beneath the Surface ." 15 June 1998. people.com/people/archive People Magazine Article . 18 February 2013.

THE MAN TURNED INTO A CELEBRITY BY A CRIME OF PASSION: JOHN WAYNE BOBBITT

Crimes of passion usually destroy their victims, but that wasn't the case for John Wayne and Lorena Bobbitt. The violent and dysfunctional couple were transformed into a pair of B-list celebrities by a night of passion and violence. John Wayne Bobbitt even enjoyed a career as a porn star because of a violent attack on him by his wife.

What started out as a normal husband and wife quarrel between the two became both a medical miracle and a media circus. It also made John Wayne Bobbitt at least briefly one of the most recognizable men in America and a household name to this day.

An Act of Unspeakable Violence Makes a Celebrity

The Bobbitts' fame began with a horrific act that captured the imagination of people throughout the world. On the night of June 23, 1993, John Wayne Bobbitt, an ex-Marine and something of a failure, came home drunk. He had been out with the boys, and his wife Lorena wasn't very happy about it.

When John came into the bedroom, Lorena became enraged and told him she was going downstairs to get a glass of water. Instead she got a kitchen knife, came back upstairs, and chopped off half of John's penis. Lorena then picked up the penis, went outside, got into her car, and drove away. After driving a short distance from the couple's Manassas, Va. apartment, Lorena threw the severed penis out the window and called 911.

Incredibly, paramedics were able to locate the penis and pack it in ice. It was then taken to the hospital, where surgeons reattached it in a nine-hour operation. Both John and Lorena were arrested. Loretta was charged with assault and John with spousal rape. Lorena claimed that John had raped her before the assault.

The Media Circus Begins

Not surprisingly, the case attracted the attention of the media, particularly the tabloids. Reporters from two continents rushed to cover the trial and find out what had happened. They were helped by the fact that John Wayne Bobbitt was eager to cash in on his newfound fame.

The trial that followed in 1994 gave the media all the drama that it wanted. Lorena Bobbitt claimed that she was abused and mistreated by her husband. Among other things, she said he bragged about cheating on her and forced her to get an abortion. She was found not guilty by reason of insanity; the jury found she had severed John's penis because she had an irresistible sexual urge to hurt him. Lorena was sent to the Central State Hospital, a mental hospital, in Petersburg, Va.

John Wayne Bobbitt was found not guilty of spousal rape in 1994, although evidence at his trial indicated some of Lorena's claims about abuse were true. Whether the jury felt he was punished enough is unknown. One thing is clear, Lorena is hardly a shrinking violet, and it's difficult to picture such a violent woman putting up with four years of abuse – the couple was married in 1989.

From Victim to Shameless Self-Promoter

After the circus in the courtroom was over, John Wayne Bobbitt became a shameless self-promoter and found numerous ways to keep his fame going. He organized an unsuccessful band called the Severed Parts to pay the bills.

Then he appeared in the "adult movies" John Wayne Bobbitt: Uncut and John Wayne Bobbitt's Frankenpenis. Bobbitt's porn career wasn't very successful despite his celebrity; he even appeared on episode of World Wrestling Entertainment's hugely popular Raw broadcast in 1998.

Once Bobbittmania lost its appeal, John Wayne Bobbitt sunk back into the status of a working class loser. He moved to Las Vegas and took on a succession of decidedly unglamorous jobs, including limousine driver, tow-truck driver, pizza deliveryman, moving man, and bartender. He reportedly worked as a "minister" at a wedding chapel in the city, and some news reports indicate that Bobbitt also worked at the Mustang Ranch, a brothel in Northern Nevada.

Bobbittmania

The Bobbitts soon became part of pop culture and even the political debate. Feminists turned Lorena into a heroine and glorified her as a victim of domestic violence that fought back. Others noted that men could be victims of domestic violence.

Intriguingly, the case also became part of the language, as terms like "Bobbittised punishment" and "The Bobbitt Procedure" became widely used. The couple also became a popular target for standup comedians and satirists.

Still Trying to Cash in After all these Years

Lorena Bobbitt, who is now going by her maiden name of Lorena Gallo, maintained a much lower profile. She worked at a beauty shop and did such a good job avoiding the media spotlight that an urban legend that she had been killed in a car accident became popular. In reality, Lorena was working in a beauty salon in the Washington, DC area and operating a charity that helps victims of domestic abuse. She also had a relationship with a man named David Bellinger and gave birth to a daughter.

Lorena's only reported run-in with the law was a 1997 assault charge. Media reports indicate that Lorena had hit her mother while watching television. She was acquitted of that charge.

In 2009, John Wayne Bobbitt and Lorena Gallo were reunited on the Oprah Winfrey show. At the time, media outlets reported that John Wayne Bobbitt was interested in getting back together with his ex-wife, but Lorena wasn't interested. Since then, the two have stayed out of the media spotlight.

The Copy Cat Legend

Since the height of Bobbittmania, an urban legend about copycat crimes in which women cut off penises has spread. Several such incidents have been reported, but there is no evidence that they are related to the Bobbitt affair. Instead, the media seems to be using the sensational case to hype other crimes because the Bobbitts still sell newspapers 20 years later.

Bibliography

The Telegraph . "John Wayne Bobbitt reunited with wife 16 years she sliced off his penis ." 5 May 2009. telegragh.co.uk. Daily Telegraph Newspaper Article . 19 February 2013.

Wikipedia . "John and Lorena Bobbitt ." n.d. en.wikipedia.org. Online Encyclopedia Entry. 19 February 2013.

THE STRANGE DEATH OF ARTUNO GATTI: WAS IT A CRIME OF PASSION OR SUICIDE?

Crimes of passion are often messy affairs in which no easy answers or clear motives are available. Sometimes it isn't even possible to tell if an actual crime took place or not. Such a case involves the death of welterweight and featherweight world champion boxer Arturo Gatti in 2009.

Gatti's body was found in a hotel room in Porto de Galinhas, Brazil, on July 12, 2009, when he was reportedly on a second honeymoon. Brazilian authorities concluded that Gatti, who had a history of suicide attempts, mental health problems, and substance abuse, had hanged himself. Gatti's friends and family contend that he was murdered by his wife, Amanda Rodriquez, or somebody working with her in order to inherit his estate.

The case was clouded by feuding over Gatti's estate; at the time of his death, he reportedly had two wills. One left all of his money to Rodriguez and her son Arturo Gatti Jr., while another left the money to Gatti's mother and other family members.

A Crime of Passion or Cold-Blooded Murder?

Gatti's death might have been a crime of passion because he and Amanda had apparently been fighting the night before. It might have been a cold-blooded murder because it is difficult to see how an average-sized woman could have hanged a professional boxer. Gatti reportedly pushed Rodriguez to the ground in the street outside the hotel on the night of July 11.

Gatti's marriage was a tumultuous one; friends reported that he and Amanda were constantly arguing. She often sent him long text messages filled with angry rants. There were also documented cases of physical abuse.

Yet the death might have been a cold-blooded murder because Gatti might have been planning to cut Rodriguez out of his will at the time of his death. Gatti's family was trying to get him to leave Amanda at the time of the murder. Rodriguez might have lured Gatti to Brazil (her native country) in order to murder him there.

Conflicting Accounts and Confusing Police Reports

Part of the reason for the mystery is the confusing behavior of Brazilian police. Investigators first concluded the death was a murder and arrested Rodriguez. Then they released her and declared it a suicide.

Gatti's manager, Pat Lynch, wasn't convinced by the police claims. He hired a private detective named Paul Ciolino to look into the matter. Ciolino issued a 300-page report that concluded the investigation of Gatti's death was "inadequate." Like the police, Ciolino was unable to conclusively determine the cause of Gatti's death, although they told the press that it was a homicide. Brazilian authorities ignored the private investigation.

A second autopsy performed in Gatti's hometown of Montreal further clouded the situation. The Canadian coroners concluded that Gatti had suffered injuries that the Brazilian investigators had ignored.

A Crime of Passion or a Broken Heart?

Another possible motive for Arturo Gatti Sr.'s death was proposed by sportswriter Chris Jones. Jones believes that Gatti simply had nothing left to live for after the end of his boxing career. Gatti's last fight was on July 14, 2007, less than two years before his death. The fight took such a toll on Gatti that he announced his retirement in his dressing room right after the match.

Gatti's boxing career was certainly a brutal one that took a terrible toll on his body. He won fights and the admiration of fans by boxing with broken hands and swollen eyes. Gatti may have suffered head injuries as well; his face was often covered with blood after fights. The "fight to the bitter end" attitude that made Gatti a fan favorite may have led to his death.

Gatti was most famous for his three fights against Micky Ward, the boxer made famous by Mark Wahlberg's movie The Fighter. Media reports indicate that Wahlberg is planning a sequel to that film that will feature Gatti as a character.

Mental Problems and Crimes of Passion

A strong possibility is that Arturo Gatti might have suffered brain damage in the ring. It is known that professional fighters can suffer brain damage that leads to suicide and other violent behaviors. Arturo Gatti fought in 49 professional fights and he suffered technical knockout (TKO) losses in his last two fights.

Outside the ring, Gatti had a long history of heavy drinking and drug abuse. The drinking and drug abuse might have increased the brain damage. Gatti also threatened to commit suicide in 2004 and may have attempted suicide by overdosing in 2006.

An Unsolved Mystery

The death of Arturo Gatti will probably remain an unsolved mystery. None of the investigations have been able to determine a conclusive cause of death, although circumstantial evidence points to suicide. It is unclear if the dispute over the wills and Gatti's estate was ever resolved. Gatti's fame will live on; he was inducted into the International Boxing Hall of Fame in 2012.

Bibliography

CBC News. "Arturo Gatti's suicidal past re-vealed ." 23 September 2011. cbc.ca/news/canada . Summary of Fifth Estate news broadcast. 20 February 2013.

ESPN.com news services . "Foul play sus-pected in Gatti's death." 11 July 2009. sports.espn.go.com. Wire Service News Article . 20 February 2013.

Jones, Chris. "The Odd Death of Arturo Gatti." 22 August 2011. grantland.com. Online Editorial Column. 20 February 2013.

Longhini, Doug. "How did boxer Arturo Gatti die?" 24 March 2012. cbnews.com. 48 Hours Investigation . 20 February 2013.

Wikipedia. "Arturo Gatti ." n.d. en.wikipedia.org. Online Encyclopedia Entry . 20 February 2013.

THE WOMAN WHO WAS MURDERED WITH A PARACHUTE: ELS VAN DOREN

Nothing is safe when you get involved in a love triangle that includes an obsessed rival for a lover. A Belgian woman named Els Van Doren found that out the hard way when she and another member of her parachute club fell in love with the same man.

The rival, who in a bizarre coincidence, was also named Els (Els Clottemans), sabotaged Van Doren's parachute, which caused her to fall 13,000 feet to her death. To add to the terrifying scenario, Van Doren unwittingly filmed her own murder with a camera attached to her helmet. The murder proves that there is almost no length to which an obsessed person might go to eliminate a rival.

Love Triangle at the Parachute Club

Els Van Doren and Els Clottemans had a lot in common. They had the same hobby skydiving and they loved the same man, Marcel Somers. Both women also had something else in common. They were married to other men while involved with Marcel Somers. Yet they had one difference: Clottemans became obsessed to the point of violence.

Like many obsessed killers, Clottemans was a seemingly normal person. She was a 26-year schoolteacher who was married with two children. Yet sometime in 2002, she started having an affair with Somers. He wasn't much of a catch; he was taking another woman, Els Van Doren, out while sleeping with Clottemans.

At some point, Somers grew tired of Clottemans and tried to break off the affair. Clottemans showed true sociopathic instincts and blamed somebody else for the collapse of her love affair. Sociopaths are egotistical and don't realize that they might be the cause of their problems. Like some obsessed individuals, Clottemans thought she could solve her problems by eliminating her rival.

Concocting a Plot for Murder

Clottemans first tried to destroy Van Doren and Somers' relationship by sending anonymous letters to Van Doren's husband. She was apparently trying to tell him about the affair. Clottemans also made anonymous phone calls to Somers (not realizing that he could probably recognize her voice). When the phone calls failed, Clottemans reportedly try to kill herself.

She then came up with a new plan that would eliminate Van Doren once and for all. She would cut her rival's parachute cord just before a jump. Their skydiving club provided a perfect setting for such a scheme. Club members regularly performed elaborate aerial maneuvers at heights up to 13,000 feet.

During such a maneuver, Van Doren would be distracted and she might not notice the cut line. Since Clottemans would also participate in the maneuver, she would not be suspected. More importantly, there would be little or no physical evidence involved. It seemed to be the perfect method of eliminating a rival without detection.

The Perfect Murder at 13,000 Feet

The plot right out of a mystery novel unfolded almost perfectly in November 2006; the club went up in the plane and Van Doren jumped out. Almost as soon as she was out of the plane, Van Doren started struggling with her parachute as she plummeted to earth at 120 miles an hour. Clottemans, who held back from the maneuver, watched the killing unfold from a distance. Witnesses said she was frantically trying to get her parachute to work as she fell.

Disturbingly, Somers was also present and watched his lover plummet to death. He too was supposed to be part of the maneuver the two were participating in.

Van Doren was killed instantly when she crashed into a garden in a small village. Clottemans thought she had gotten away with the perfect crime because there was little or no evidence linking her to the death.

One Detail Gave Her Away

Like the villain in a mystery story, Clottemans was given away by one detail. When police examined Van Doren's parachute, they discovered that the cords had been cut so there was no way to open it. Clottemans was arrested in January 2007, two months after the death.

Clottemans used a bizarre defense in which she claimed a low self-esteem and jealousy of Van Doren drove her to kill. She tried to claim that her appearance and her father's death drove her to the affair and the murder. The court ignored this, but did note Clottemans' unstable mental condition.

Els Clottemans will not be able to see Somers again for a long time. The court sentenced her to 30 years in prison. The judge paid more attention to Els Van Doren's children than to her killer and her histrionics.

Sociopathic Behavior and Love

A sociopath is a lot like a child. They demand total attention and blame others for their problems. They also lash out violently when things don't go their way. The case of Els Van Doren proves why it is a good idea to stay away from such a person.

Bibliography

Daily Mail Reporter. "Murder at 13,000ft: The dramatic final moments of skydiving victim captured by her OWN camera." 26 September 2010. dailymail.co.uk. Daily Mail Newspaper Article. 23 February 2013.

—. "Skydiver who cut straps of love rival's parachute jailed for 30 years for her murder." 21 October 2010. dailymail.co.uk . Daily Mail Newspaper Article . 23 February 2013.

Parker, Nick. "'Chute sabotage love rival caged." 21 October 2010. thesun.co.uk. The Sun newspaper article. 23 February 2013.

www.ingramcontent.com/pod-product-compliance
Lightning Source LLC
Chambersburg PA
CBHW020300030426
42336CB00010B/837